Underfoot

Underfoot

Niillas Holmberg

Illustrated by Inga-Wiktoria Påve

Translated by Jennifer Kwon Dobbs & Johanna Domokos

WHITE PINE PRESS / BUFFALO, NEW YORK

White Pine Press
P.O. Box 236
Buffalo, NY 14201
www.whitepine.org

Copyright © 2022 by Niillas Holmberg

Graphic work by DAT, www.dat.net. This book was originally published
in Sámi 2018 by DAT, Guovdageaidnu, Norway.

Translation copyright © 2022 by Jennifer Kwon Dobbs
                            and Johanna Domokos

Illustrations copyright © 2022 by Inga-Wiktoria Påve

Publication of this book was supported by a grant from the National
Endowment for the Arts, which believes that a great nation deserves
great art; with the financial assistance of FILI – Finnish Literature
Exchange; and the Witter Bynner Foundation for Poetry.

Printed and bound in the United States of America.

ISBN 978-1-945680-55-7
Library of Congress Control Number: 2022930214

Underfoot

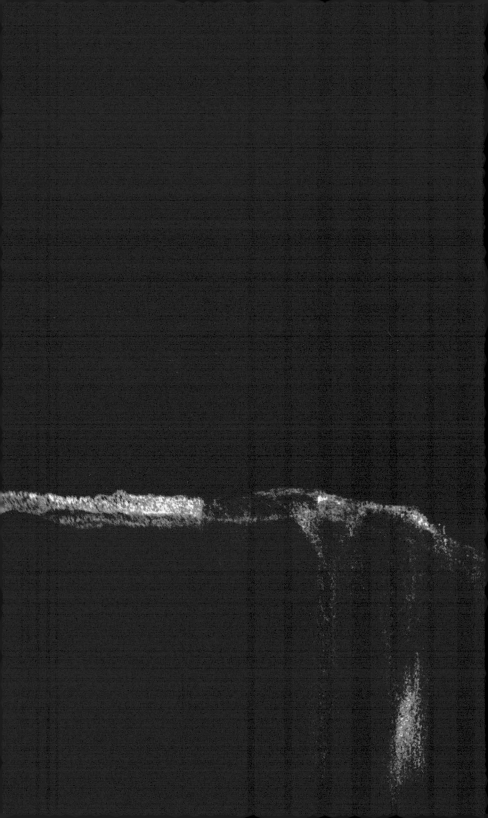

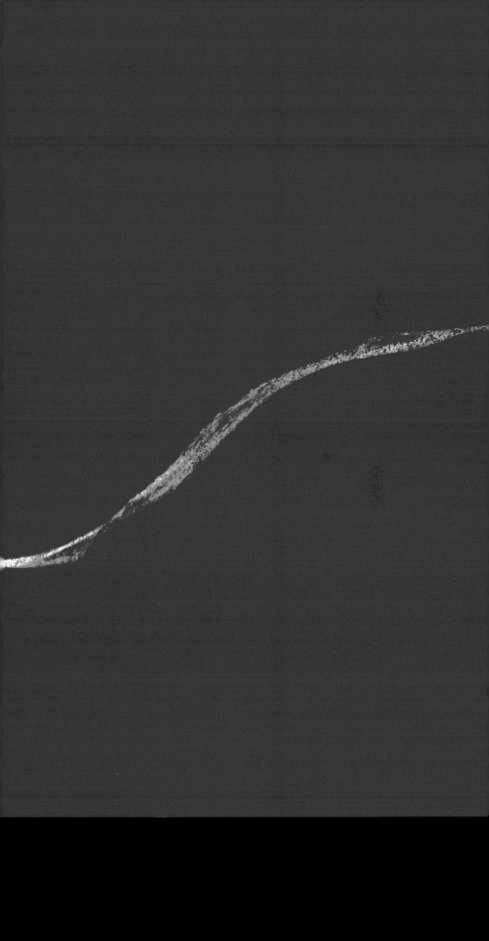

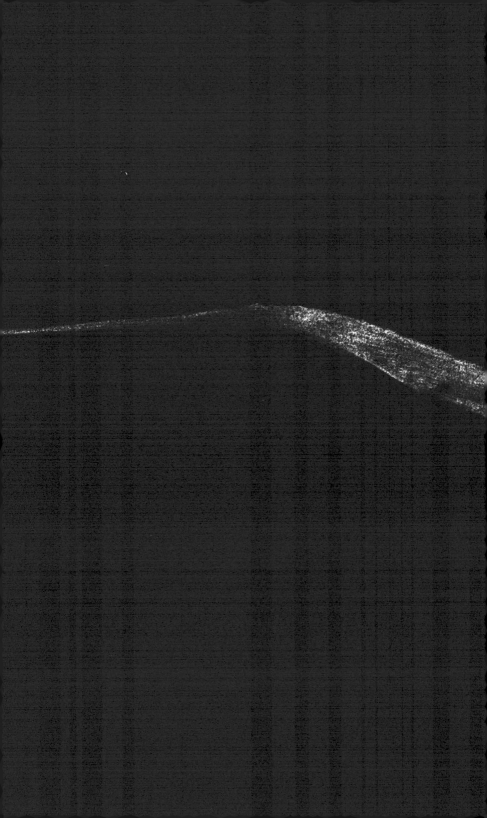

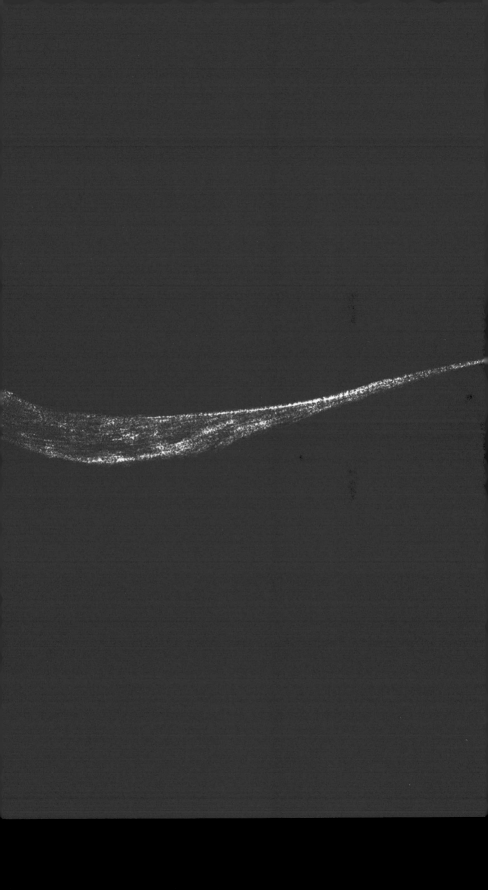

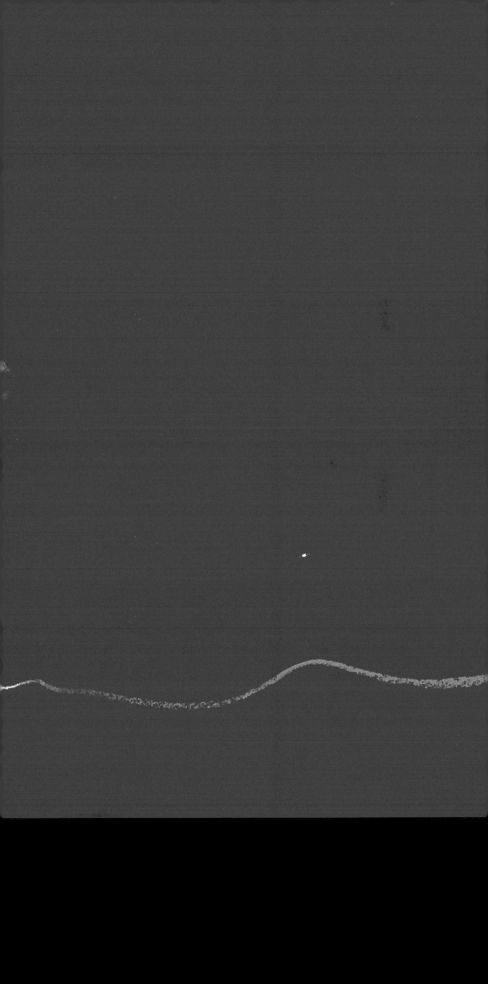

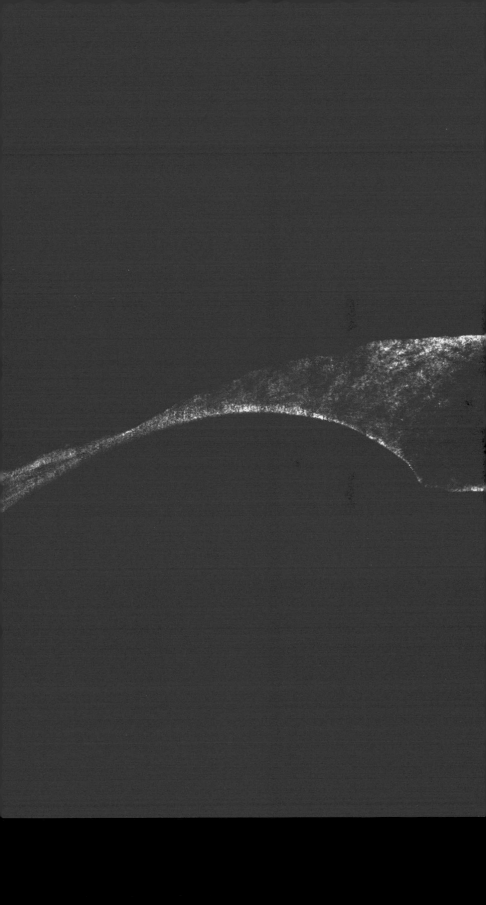

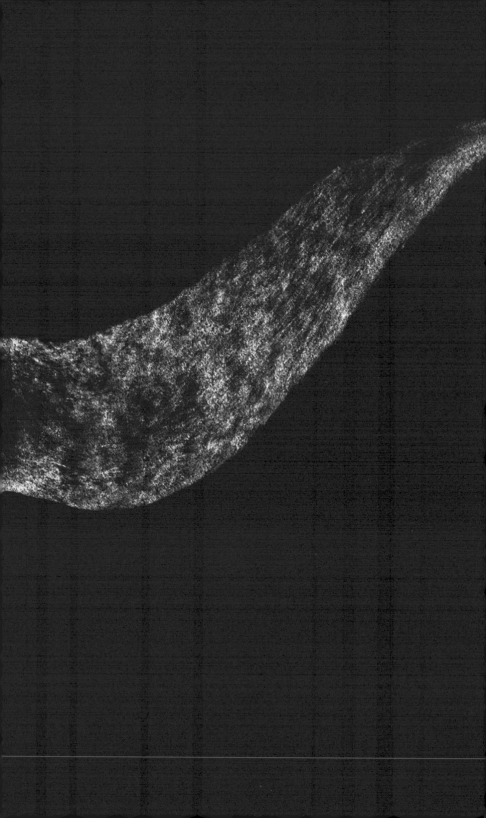

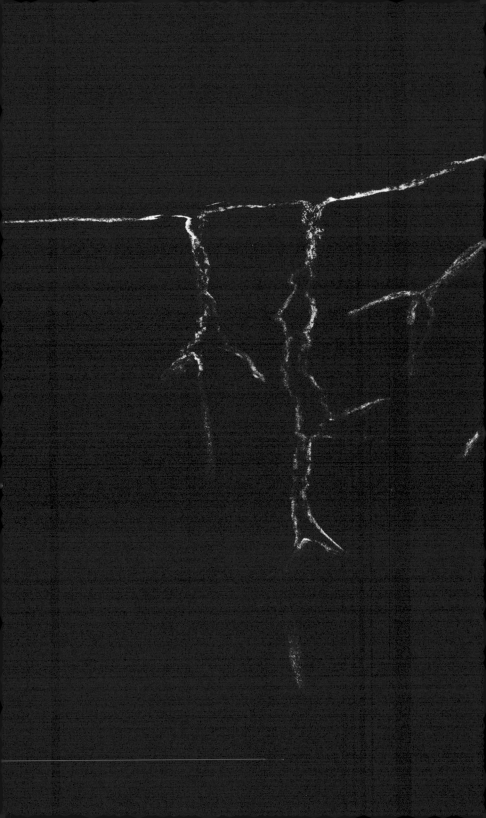

The sky thickens
trees bear the flurry, the three-winged haste.
Birches like the parents of young children
   hide traces, incubate a misleading question
      back inside its shell.

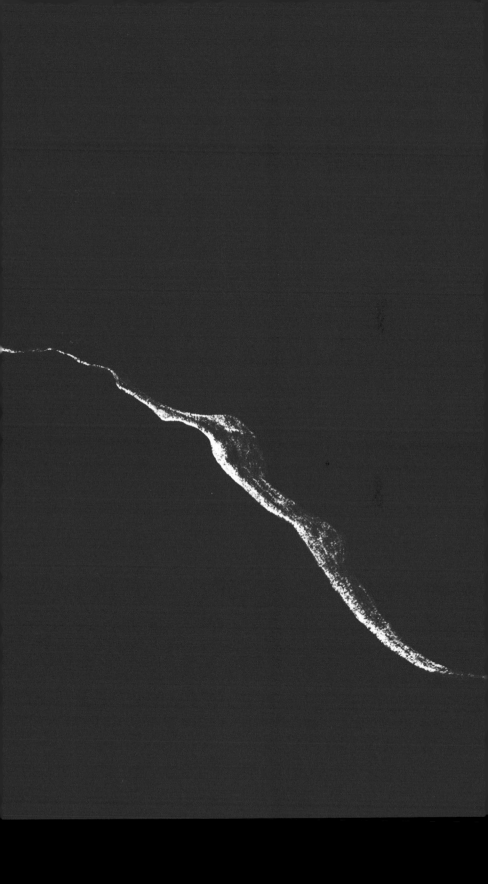

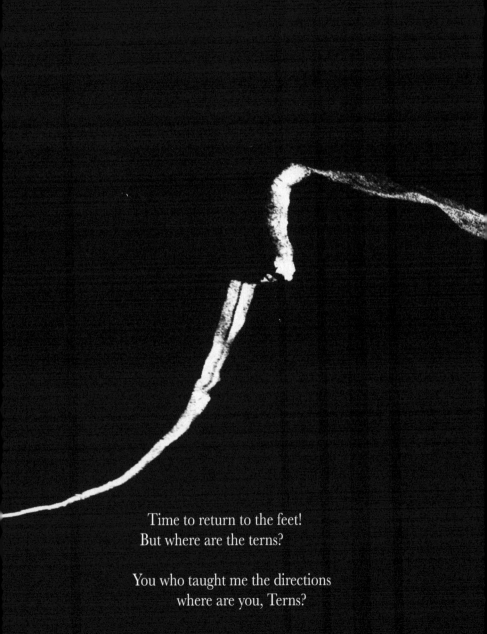

Time to return to the feet!
But where are the terns?

You who taught me the directions
where are you, Terns?

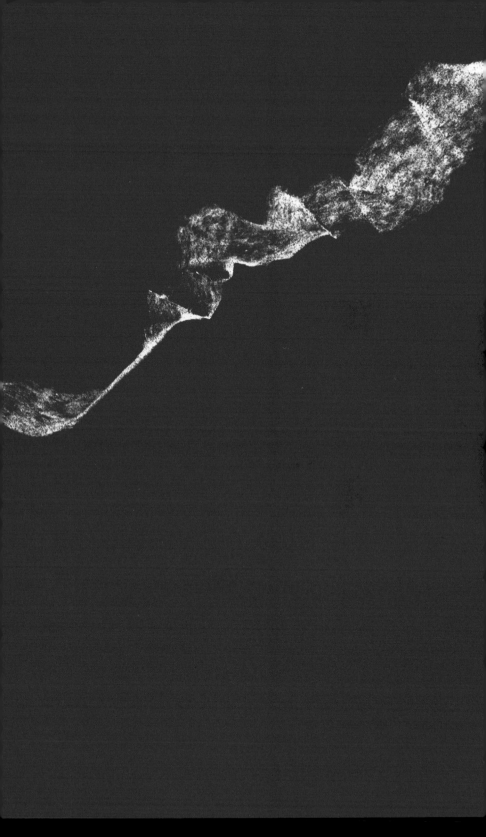

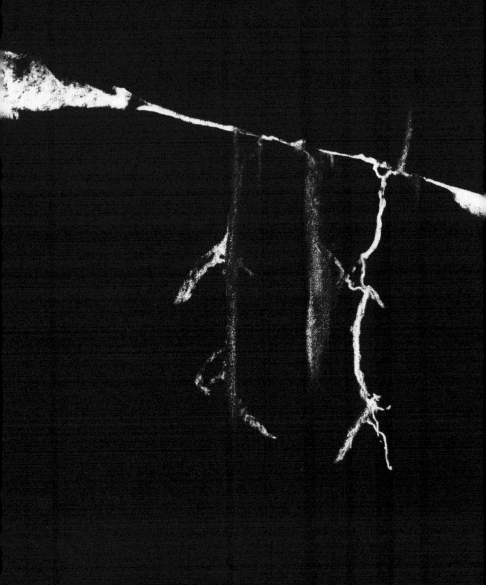

A wooden leg
  one can tell by the tracks.

  But memory, the body's memory
of reaching steps, of a linguistic
nervous system and rivers rich in fish.

  Why offer a wooden leg to a woodpecker?

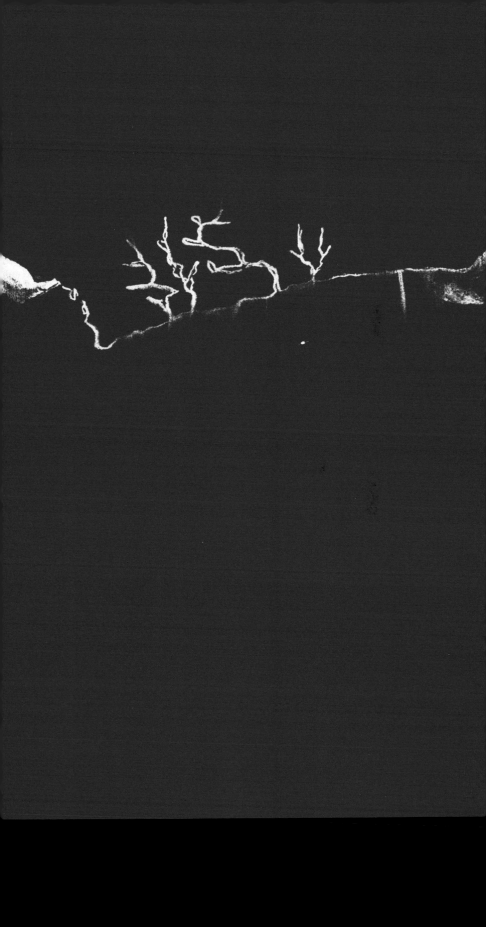

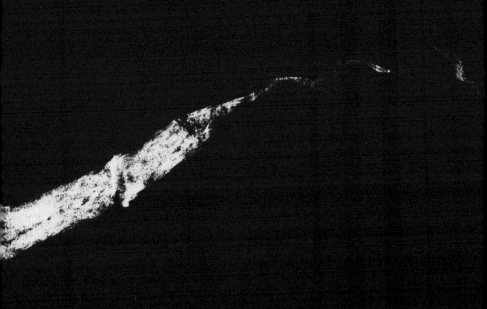

Is it too late to raise a child
or merely too late to ask?

This must be one of those gravities
the young must know the grown to grow
or when to scratch their heads.

Looking through the shoemaker's window
is to mourn stones that can't fly.

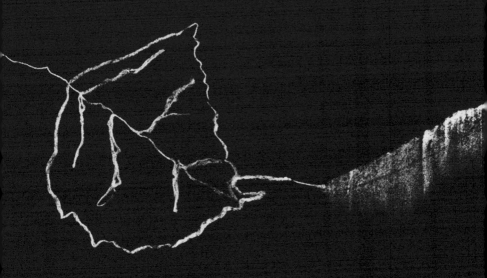

Barren birches
 fallen rights conceal the land

a rake's tooth cracks under a boot.

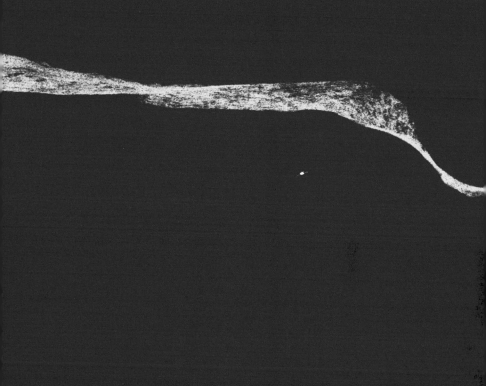

But yet they rise, children
with ears like leaves, children
with grammar hidden in their bodies.

A tactic of bluebells
proves every word is an adjective.

Look at the meadow the strategy.

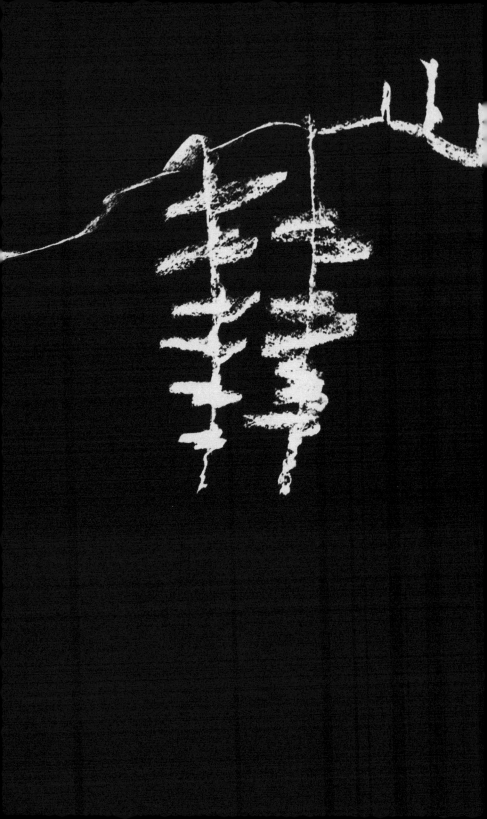

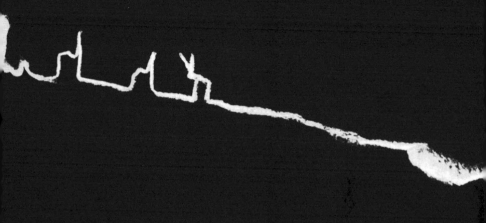

Sense the touching, trace where the body meets earth, see
the foot, ask it to speak, the heel becomes a matriarch

summoning the commission of melt and flood, and as the tern
rips the sole off the boot, a drum is born
and Oneness Verbs.

If the shoemaker protests (stones don't fly!)
challenge him to prove it barefoot
and even if he fixes the boot, it is known
you took responsibility.

Prepare to be called to negotiate, prepare to refuse
prepare, don't wait for spring

spring awaits.

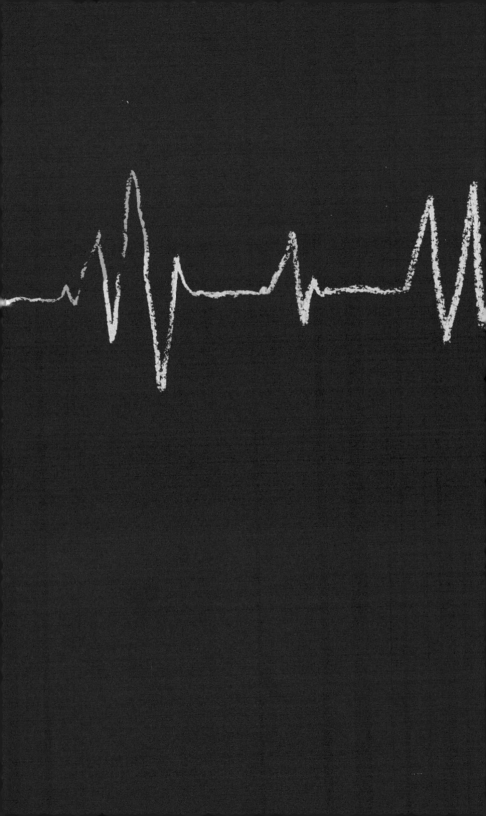

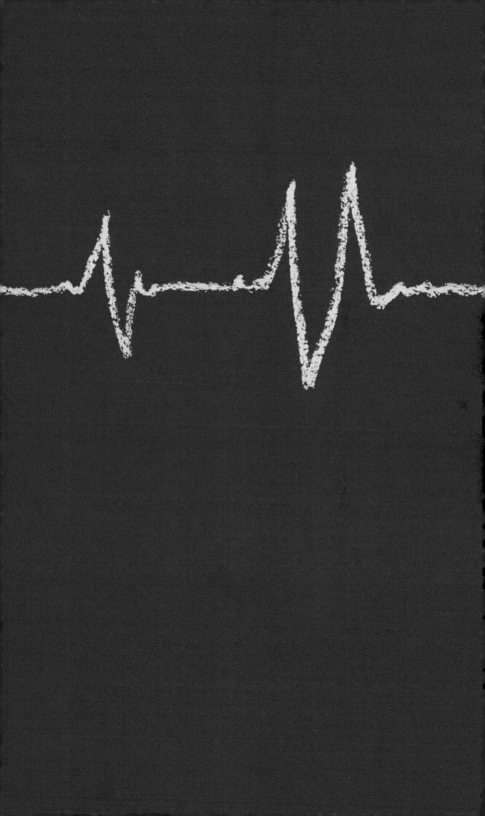

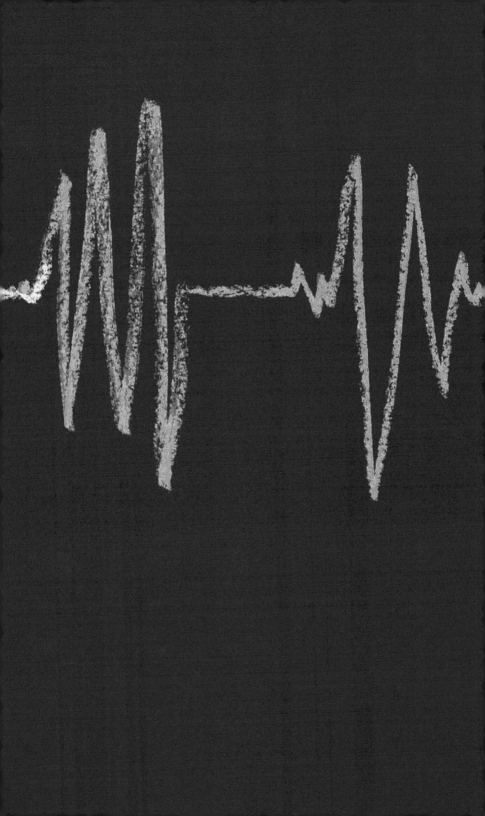

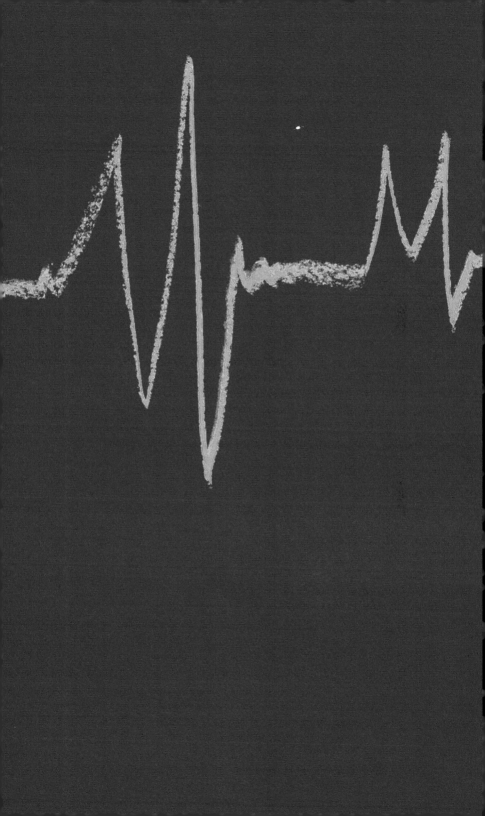

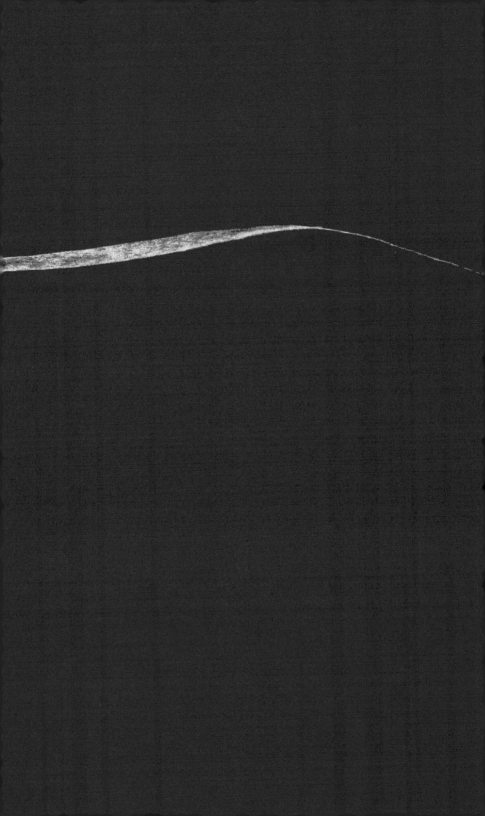

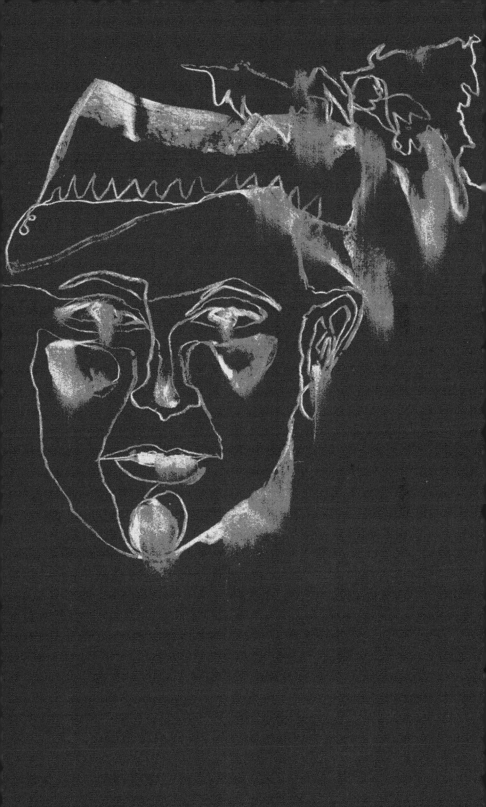

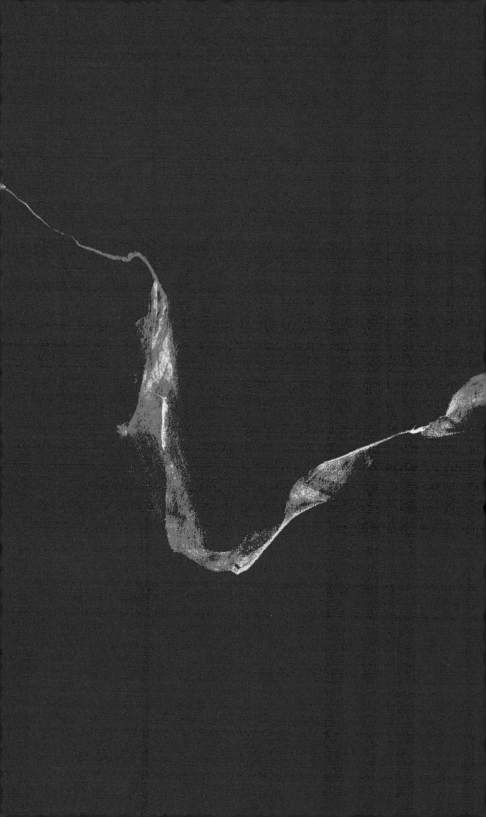

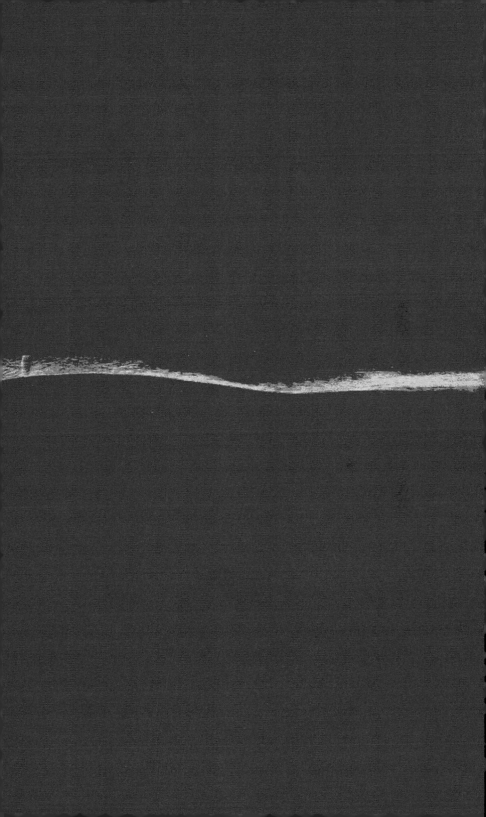

If you seek a verb
   the shoemaker is your foe.

   But can we judge the followers
who were forced to feel ashamed
of their toes, were forced to produce
booted feet and for blisters
         blame the rugged land?

                  Can you call a wolf your kin?

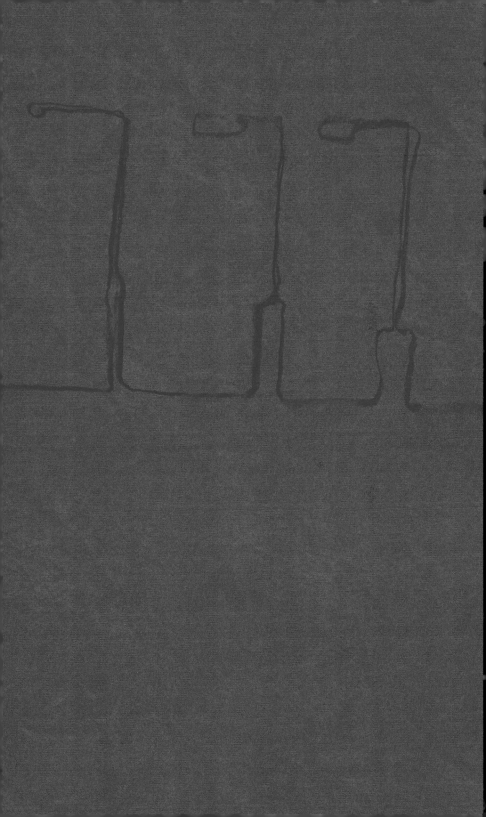

The shoe rubs, the foot festers
and oh the power we possess
to receive news about the latest boots.

Is industry trampling on bluebells?
According to the shoemaker enclosing the toes
protects both the feet and the meadows.

You see he studied the paths of life
and per his studies, the heel doesn't know
and hasn't known for centuries
its own good.

He sews the shoe with veins
nails, hair.

Yet it keeps rubbing, the foot still festers
and in the shadow of the three-winged haste
the negotiator is overtaken by night.

Before consenting to trade a wet boot
for a dry one, it is known
            a shoe can only be removed
            by ripping within.

And he fastened his eyes onto ours.

To unlock the machine, to search the needles for facts.
Which threads, stitches, seams, where, when, on what grounds?

Many set off hunting wolves
many returned howling.

Can you call a wolf your kin?

When the herd's dog
wanders off to the village or forest
the trick is to smile
when it comes back.

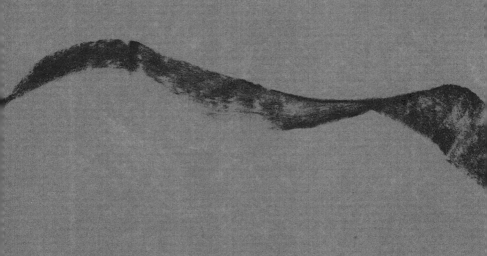

He sews veins
nails, hair.

Which verb
contains my fire? I rip as I create
wondering will they follow me
if I pierce the shoe.

A romantic paradox, my identity.

No toes, no grounds
a dog, nor a verb.

The shoemaker's children don't go barefoot—
but not even proverbs fill their shoes.

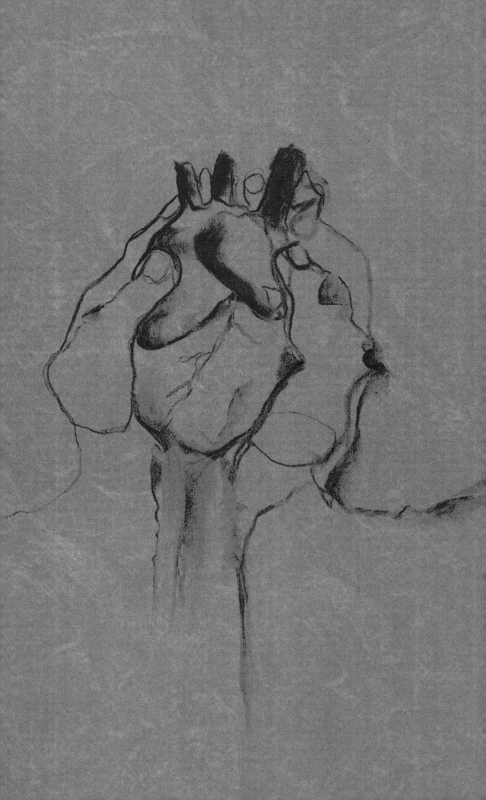

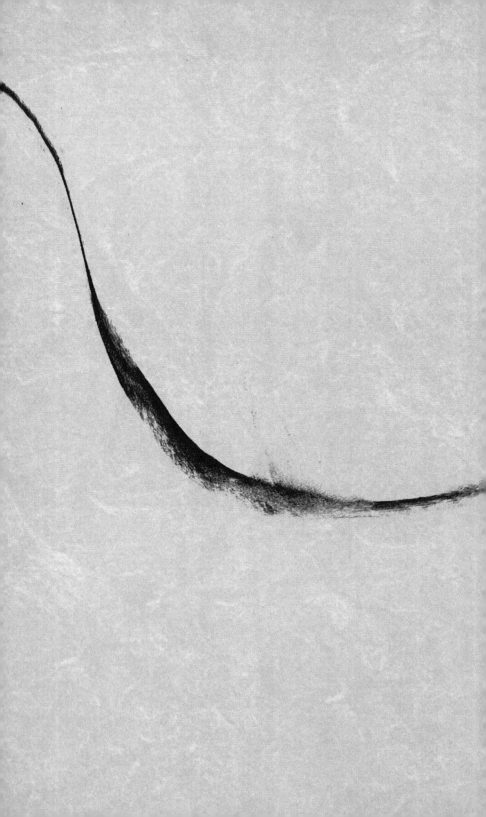

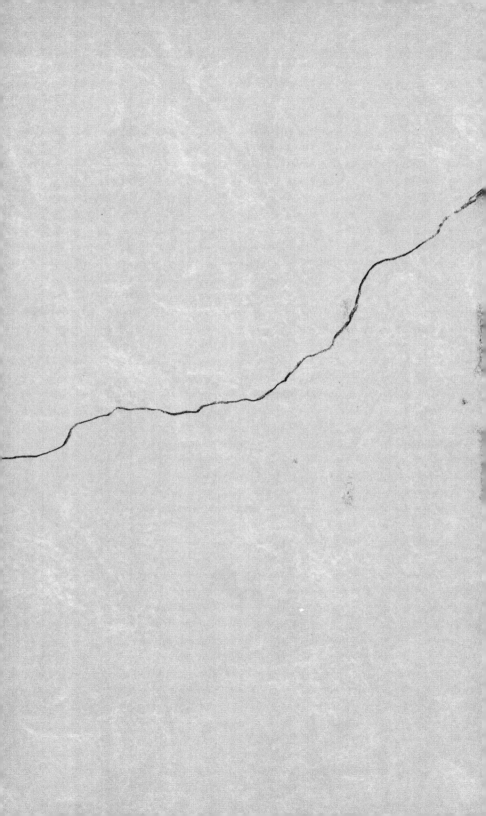

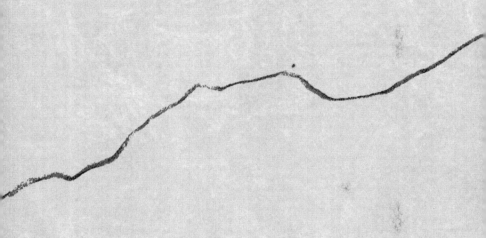

Before felling a tree, give
   a knock of warning, for the forest senses
the constellations have been patched.

Has anyone seen my present tense?
It has the humble scent of birch,
      the orange scent of smoke.   Don't leave!

      Have you seen my present tense?

Have you seen the forest?

  I'm not sure if I blushed or went pale
but among the mangy trees one shouldn't
      let the dog run.

    Forest, archive of the present perfect.

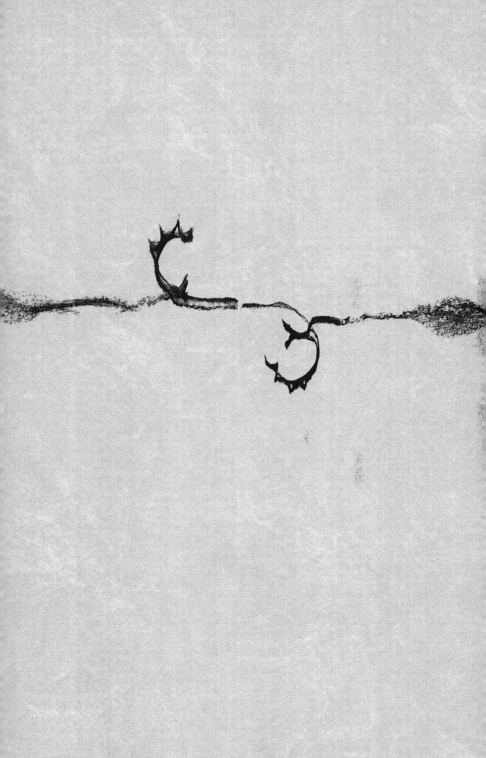

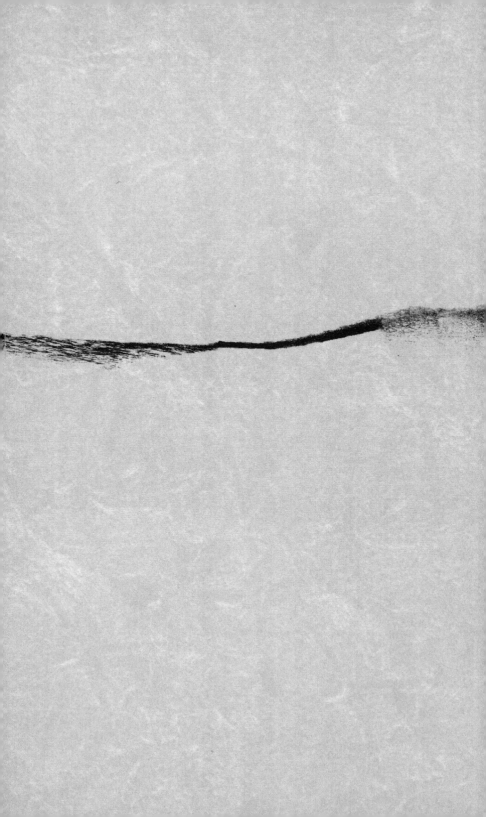

Self-reliance prohibited, walking barefoot forbidden.

Why would the shoemaker chase me
when he can criminalize my destination?

Still one awakens in the mother tongue
sea of verbs.
Should only the whale's skeleton remain
I'd still want to find it in open water.

I wish to find a quill in the sky
among the sound waves' consensus.

Get out of the murky labyrinth
      through diplomacy.
   That's what they say but some doubt.

Some believe the Minotaur, the trees and shoemaker's spawn
      swallowed the maze whole

                  and it beats in our chests
            inciting our blood to seek the sun.

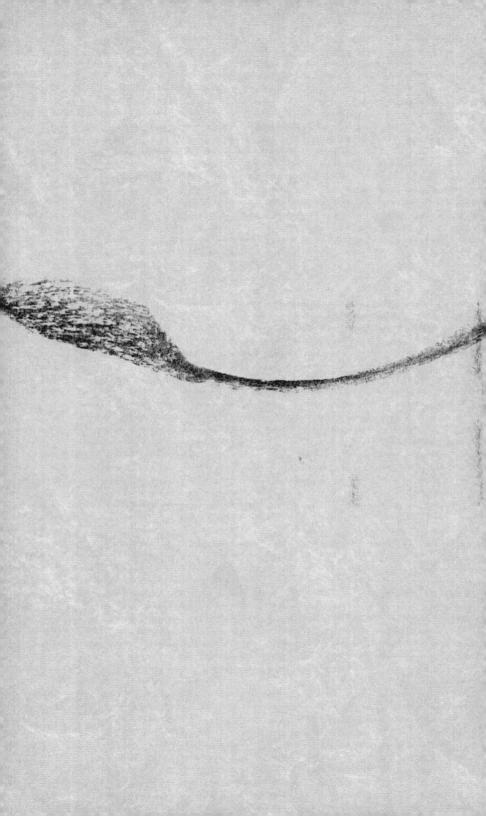

Maybe I'm wrong?
  Maybe the astronomer feeds the stars
                not vice versa.

Land reminds my hardening heel
    that it's not soft

            and my ancestors
who I'm told to denounce
to be allowed to inhabit my own land
        didn't mistake land for clouds!

Land confers on the word hunting
the namesake of asking

offers the stomach
as a reason when questioned.

But the youth became restless
and called for the road
to be repaired here and there.

By no means, said Áslat Ánde
imagine what would come.

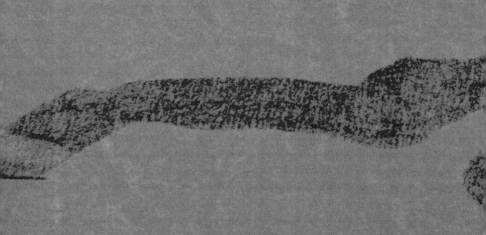

Time to return to the feet.
Underfoot there's a drum
skin carved with human letters

fortissimo

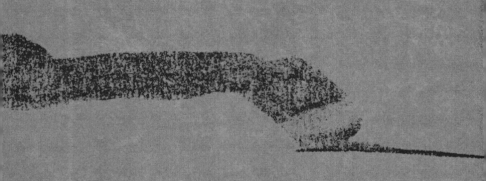

Is my care for Land more vast
　　than for the one who walks it?

Love, wide as an accordion.

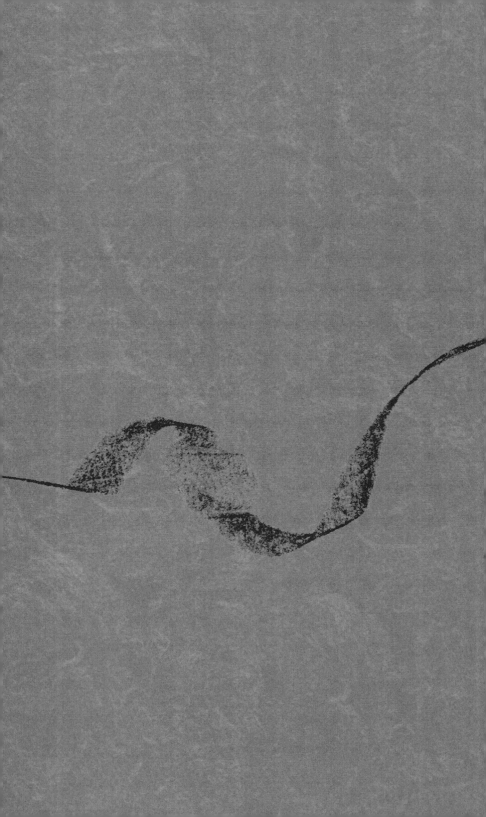

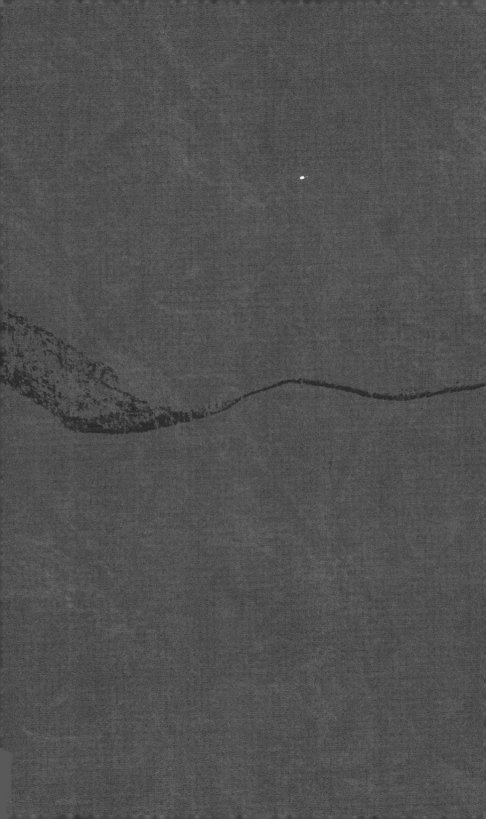

The drawn line isn't only earth and sky

but the dream of another hand.

They teach us to eat soil and seeds
     so our stomachs get beef.

Let us learn things of another sort too.

Such a child's gifts   transĕo
can manifest
by language.   translātĭo
Words would sway her
to breach borders   transfĕro
into the boundless.

And the mightiest
shapeshift   transformo
from form to form
gender to gender.   transsexualis

Studies show that a land with its language intact
is rarely decorated in funeral crepe.

Yet long ago
when a French dualist
rode into the market
            everyone raced to see his shoes.

Talk and Land
I can't keep from asking
can yearning rejoin
      Siamese twins ripped apart?

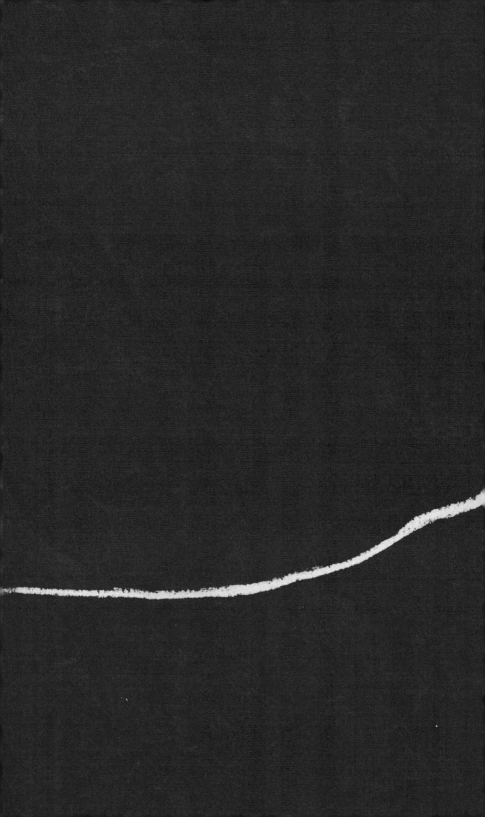

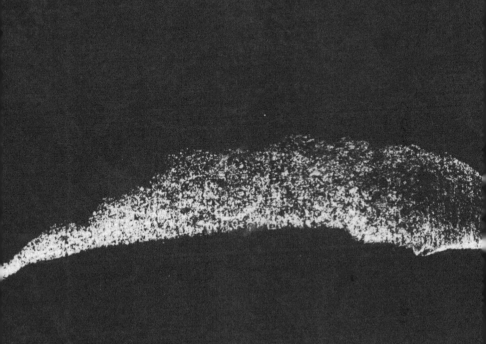

It's time for a trial
   time for Hamlet to ask To have
      or not to have rights.

Your Honor, members of the jury, good people
   I plead for the water
      to be scooped in the stream's direction.

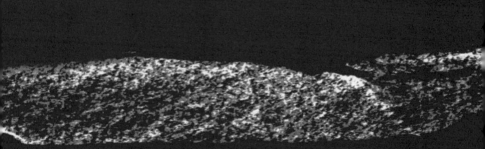

I've never been caught unaware in the dark.
As a boy I smelled the birches' branched lightning
and while we played hide-and-seek, some of us were seen
with memories of light.

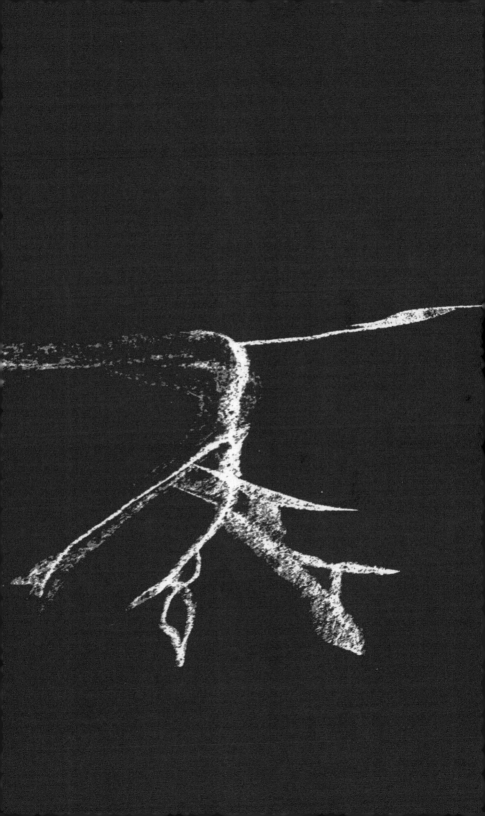

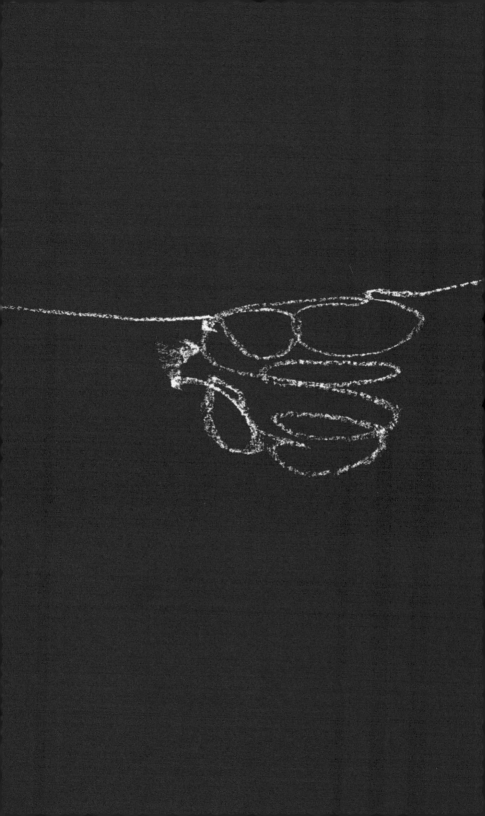

A matriarch
  gently sways in a rocking chair
  creaking like an oarlock.

      She knows what she's doing – with each stroke
        the boat floats closer, closer ...

      I ask for a story, but she's weary
      and retires like the night mist
      rising off the river.

      I tend to the fire and sit in the chair
        the boat warms me, god
          is a verb.

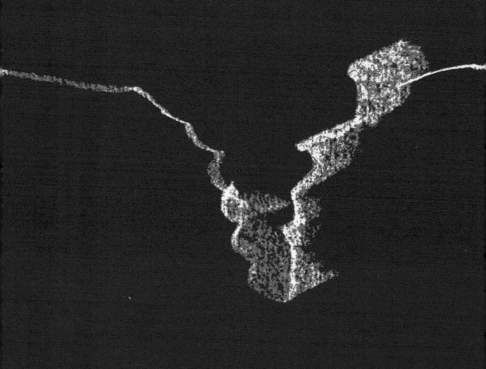

For the drums of insane asylums
    patience, forbearance.

I found a berry beneath the slush, and you know
        it tasted fine.

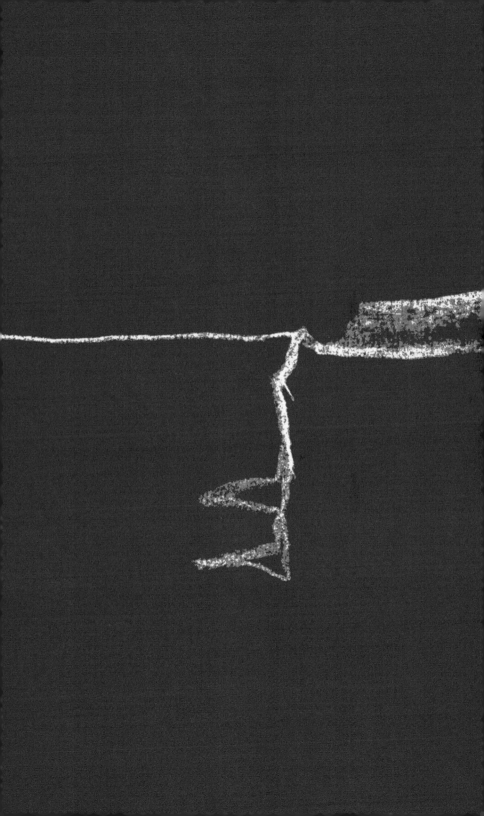

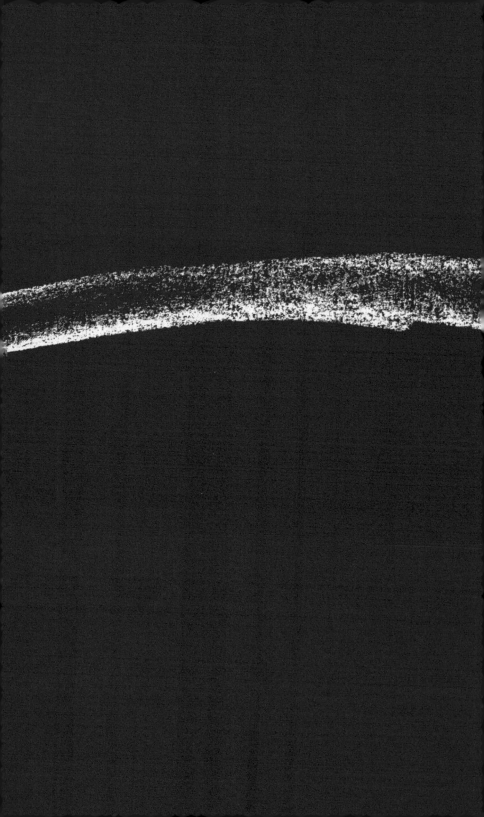

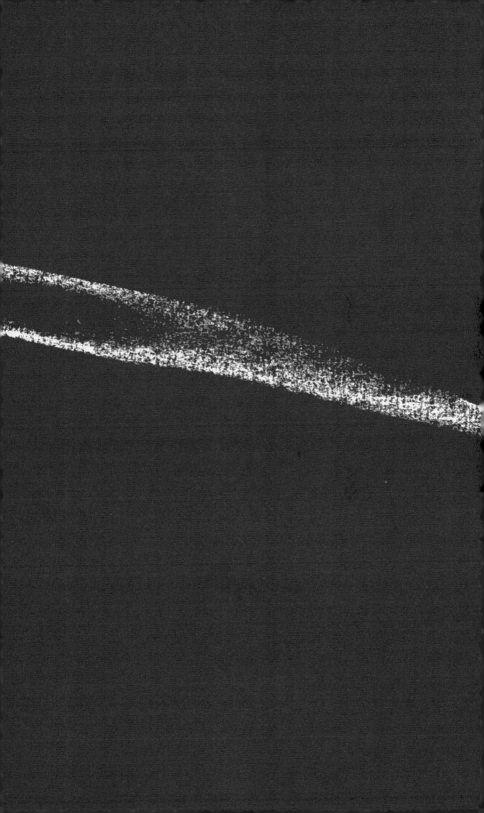

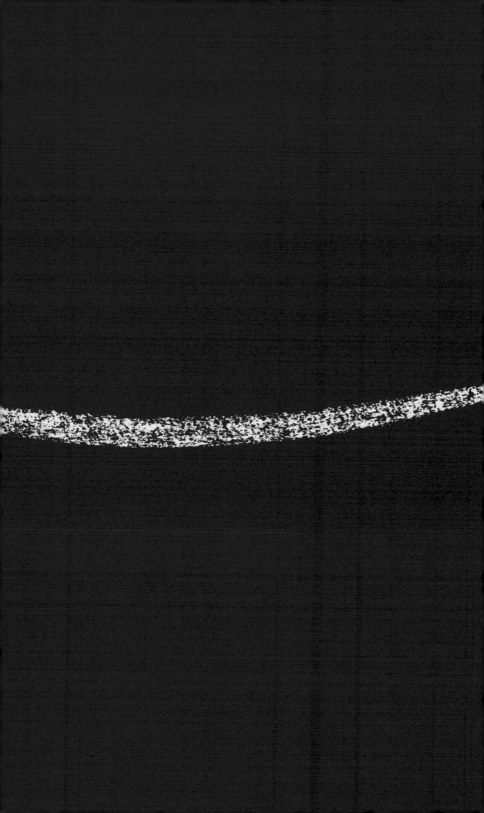

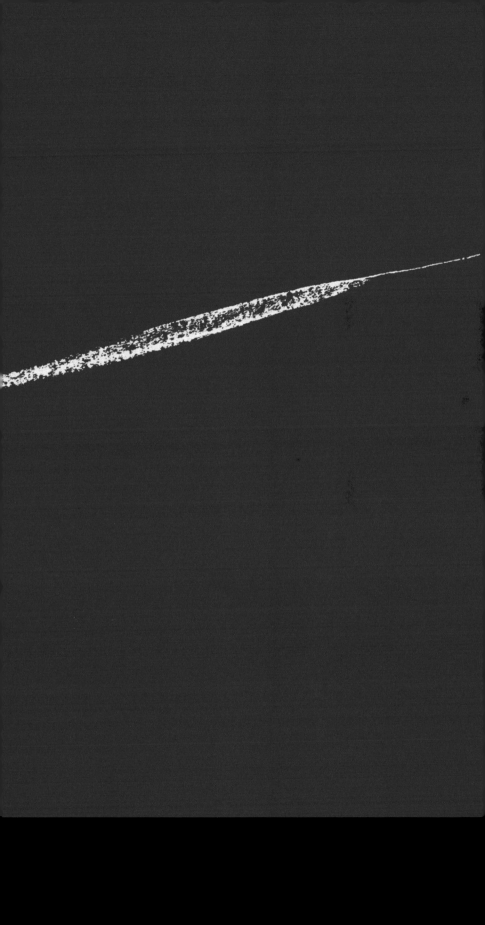

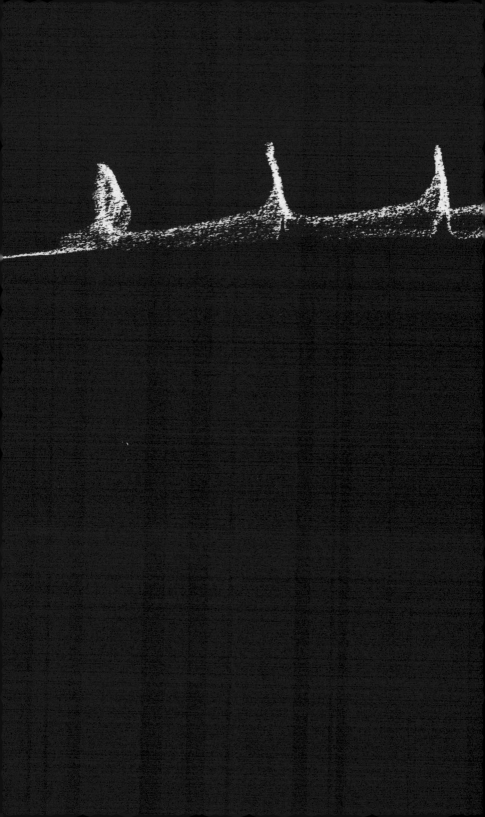

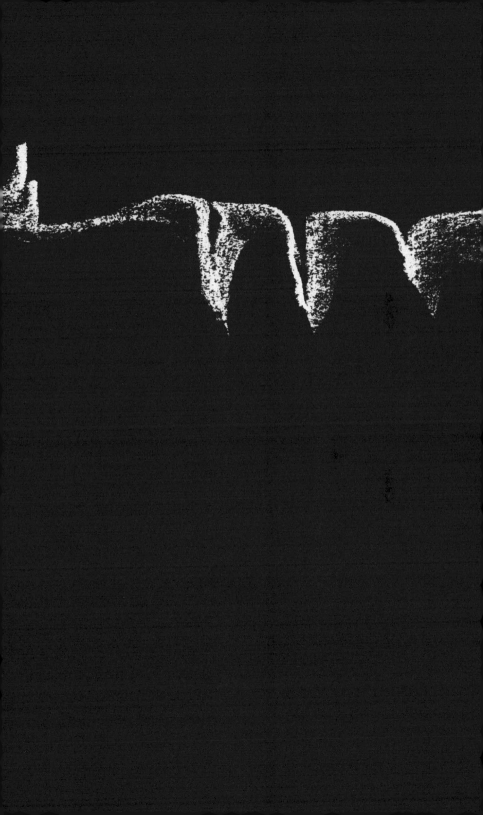

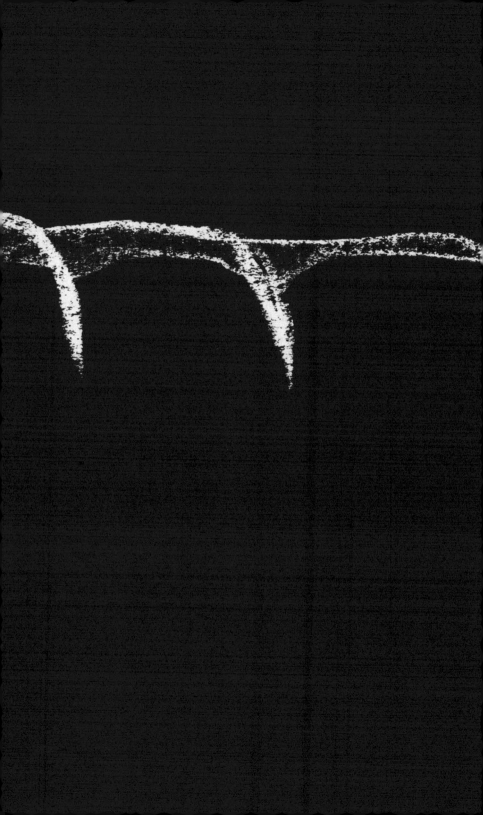

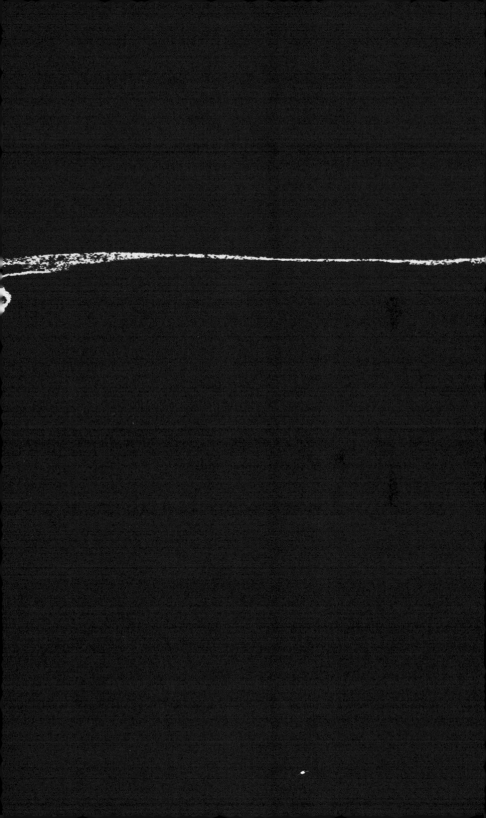

And, you find this landscape beautiful?
Thank you thank you!

To live is to answer one question.
The question is land

and I
in the best manner answer
LAND.

I describe the Land.
       Nothing describes me
       like Land.

Oh, you praise your home's scenery too.
              Strange

I've never heard anyone
       flatter themselves so much.

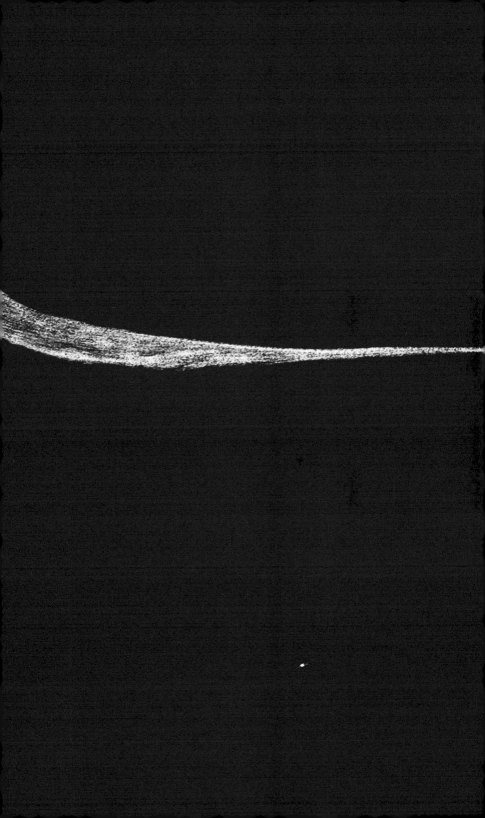

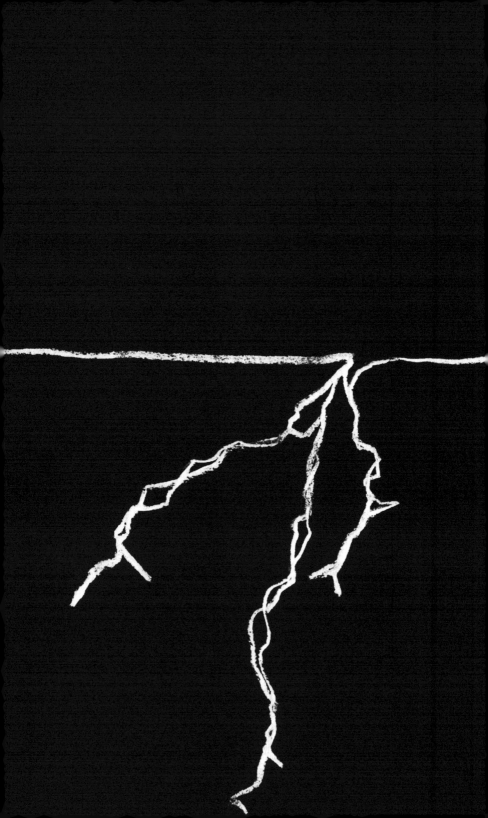

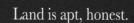

Land is apt, honest.

I'd answer aptly that apt question
but our colletive adjective stumbles.
　　The worn shoe has been patched with lies.

　　I try to imagine a shared life without lies.
　　Can a corrupt person trust
　　　　Land's signs?

Have we corrupted Land?
Let me be.

Every birch is an adjective
  every word concealed by bark.

But Land becomes ice-cold.
  What if the shoe looks nice?
What if it grows on you like a family tree?

        WHAT IF THE SHOE IS WARMER THAN THE LAND!?

            But in fall
       comparatives wither, no one
    drops leaves closer to the Land than others
            no foot lands more than another.

              Every word concealed by bark.
          Do you know the south, do you know the north?

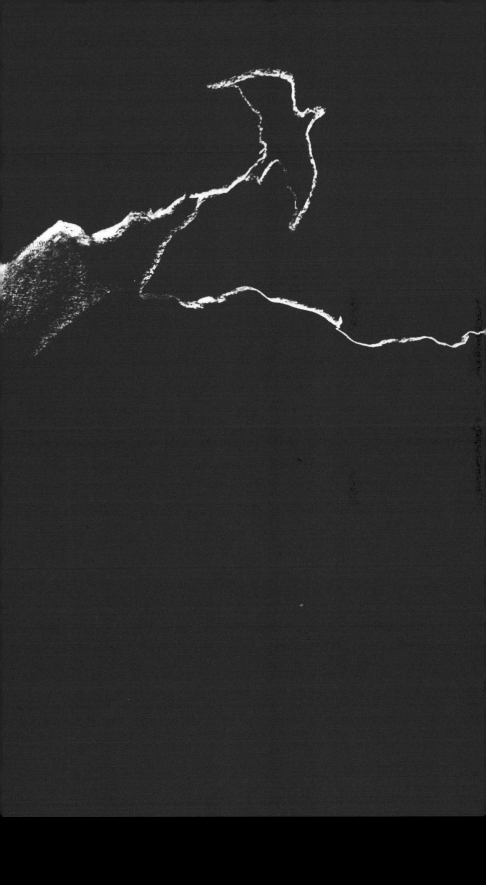

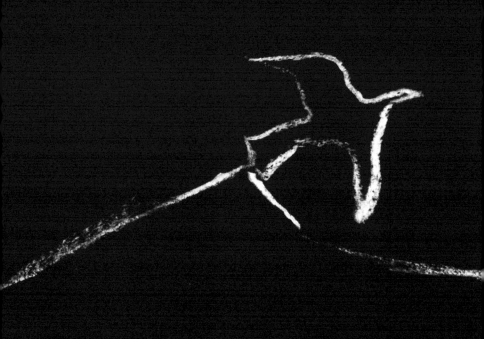

Have we really
through ourselves found in Land's nature
a corrupt feature?

If Land is lying, what is it hiding
and from whom?

Birches are bare. Who's hiding the tracks now?
How do we clear broken teeth with their own rake
and where to?

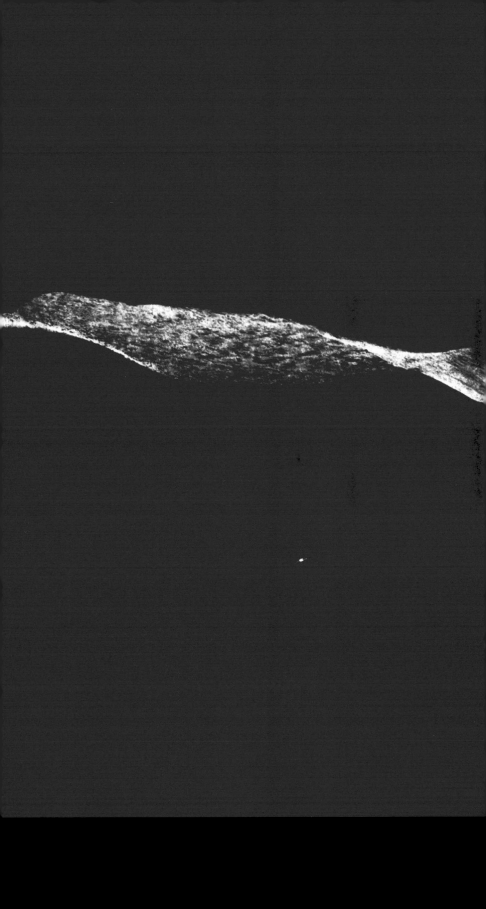

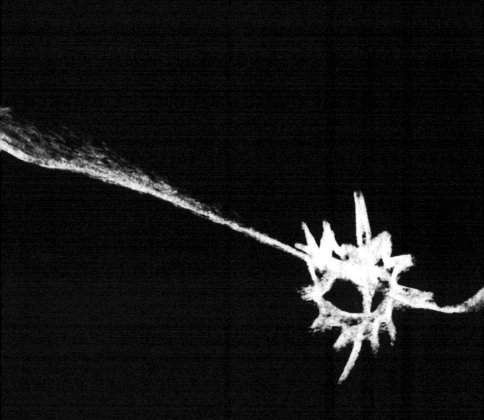

You who taught me the directions.
If I walk on foot, can these wounded eyes
    still find the angelica?

As a child I sought the company of terns.

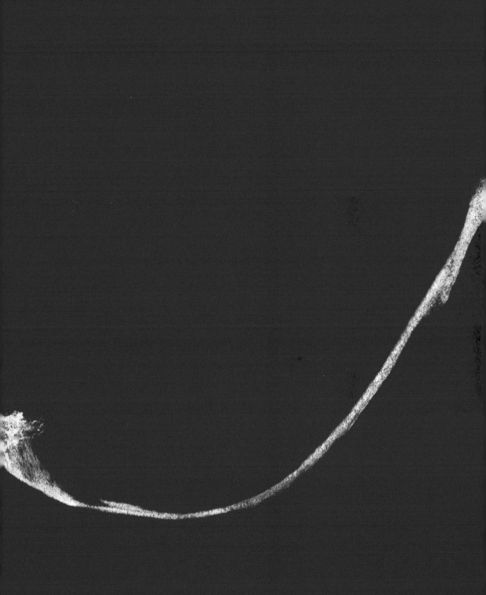

Now migrating for summer a new bird appears, the Gray Cataract –
bone for a dog or a wolf?

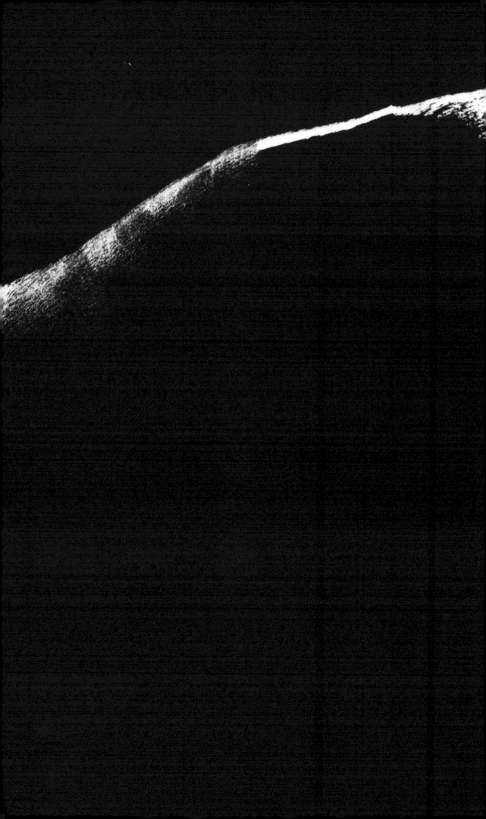

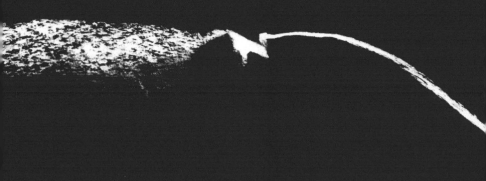

I have three wishes, but
am barely quick enough to make the first –
    you've got too many wings.

Three wings, Graybird.

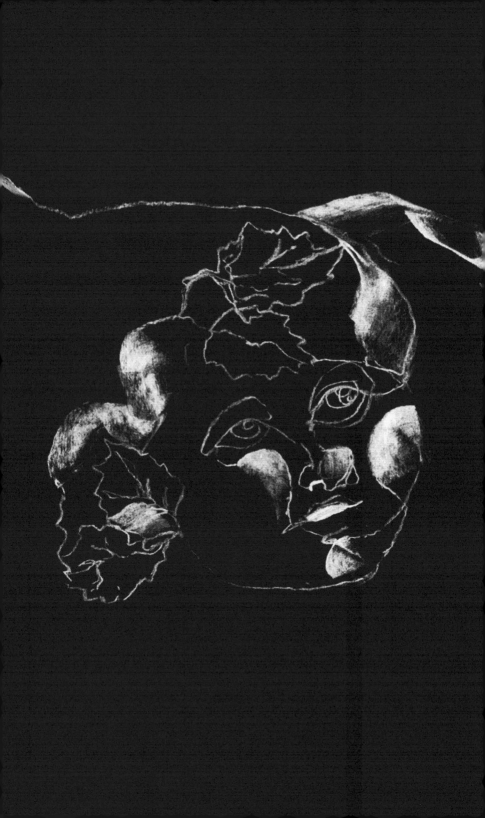

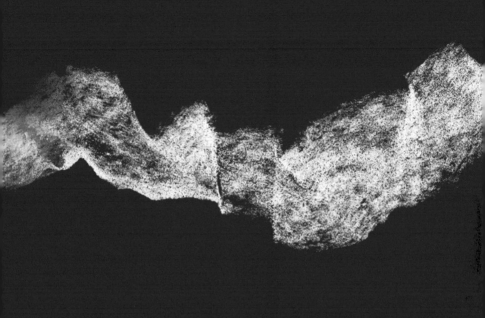

But when I began to hear the rotten shoelaces feast
    they noticed me, they tried to suppress
    their smiles as death approached.

    Could it be
the dream in which I entered the house
    and locked the door

    was about birches?

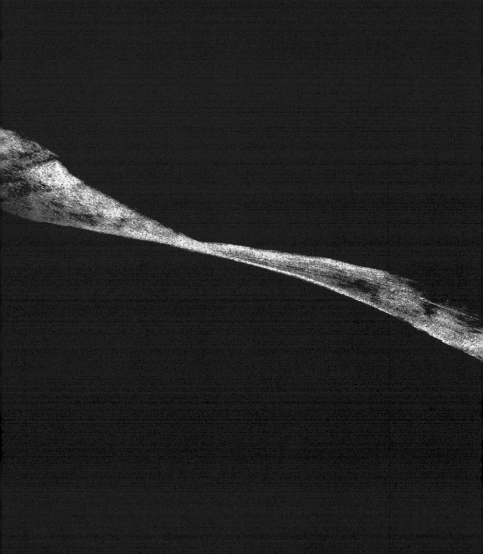

Sense the touching, trace where the body meets earth, see
the foot, ask it to speak, the heel becomes a matriarch
and Oneness Verbs.

Do I make Land corrupt?

Land.

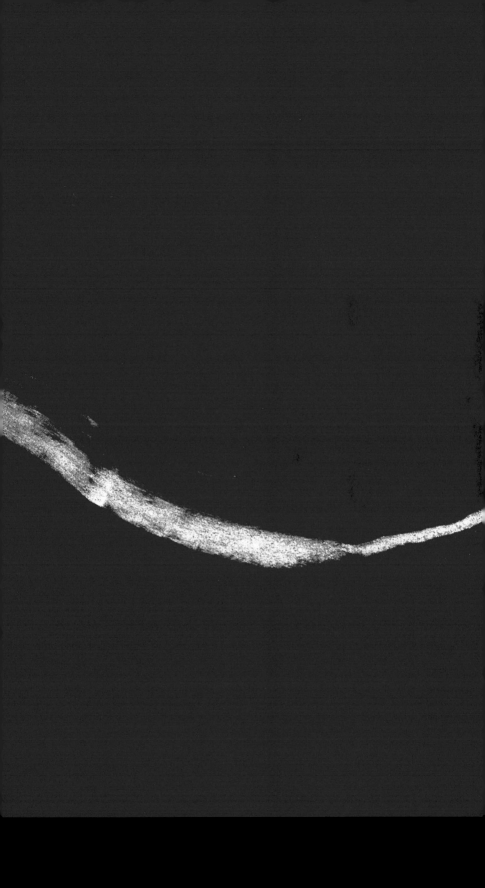

Niillas Holmberg is a Sámi writer and musician. He has written poetry collections, a novel, a feature film and essays. His works have been translated into several languages. Niillas has won awards such as the Kirsi Kunnas Poetry Award as well as being nominated for the Nordic Literature Prize twice. Niillas is known as an upfront spokesman for Sámi and indigenous rights to self-determination. He has been involved in several movements against extractivism in Sámi areas. He lives in Ohcejohka, Sámiland.

www.niillas.com

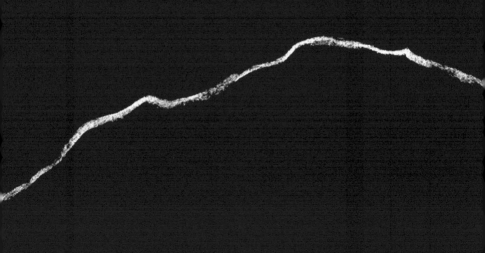

Inga-Wiktoria Påve is a Sámi visual artist and designer based in the municipality of Kiruna on the Swedish side of Sápmi. She is brought up in a traditional Sami reindeer herding community and it is from her heritage that she draws her inspiration. Påve has been exhibited amongst other places at the 2019 Ábadakone exhibition at The National Gallery of Canada in Ottawa.
www.ingawiktoriapave.com

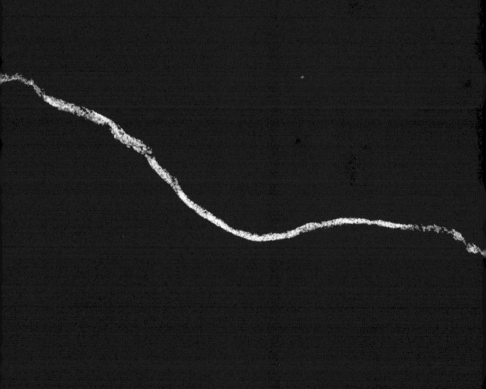

Jennifer Kwon Dobbs is the author of two poetry collections and two chapbooks, most recently *Interrogation Room*—mentioned in The New York Times—and a recipient of the Asian American Studies Book Award in Creative Writing. She is poetry editor at AGNI and professor of English at St. Olaf College.
www.jkwondobbs.com

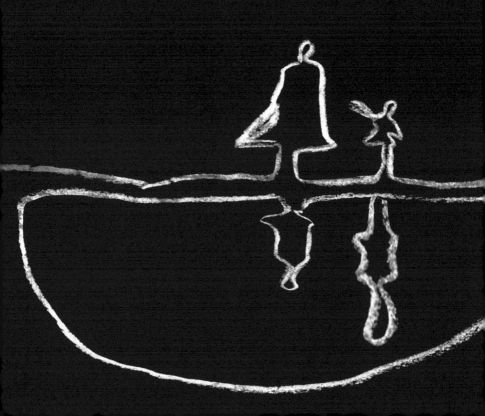

Johanna Domokos is a comparative literary scholar of indigenous cultures and minority literatures with expertise in Scandinavian and Central Europea. She is author of four monographs related to Sámi literature.

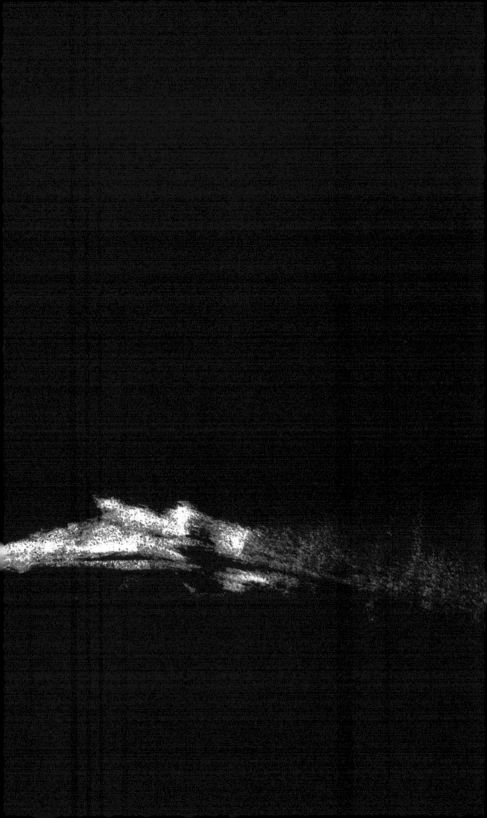

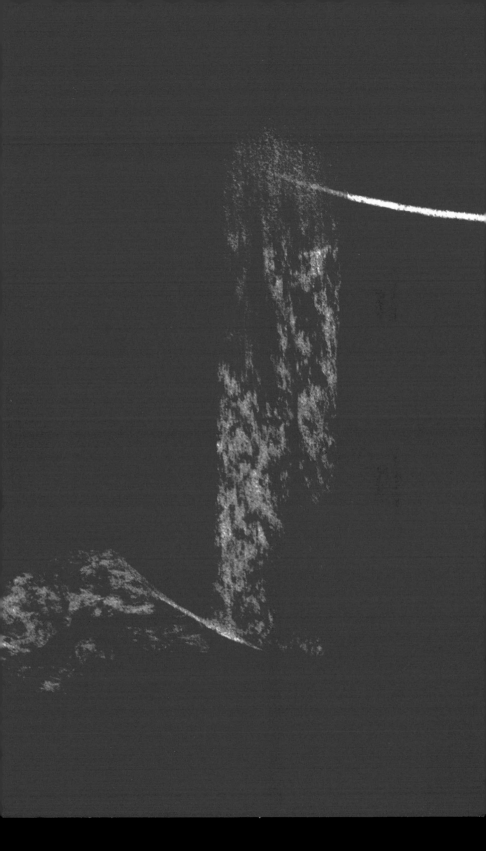

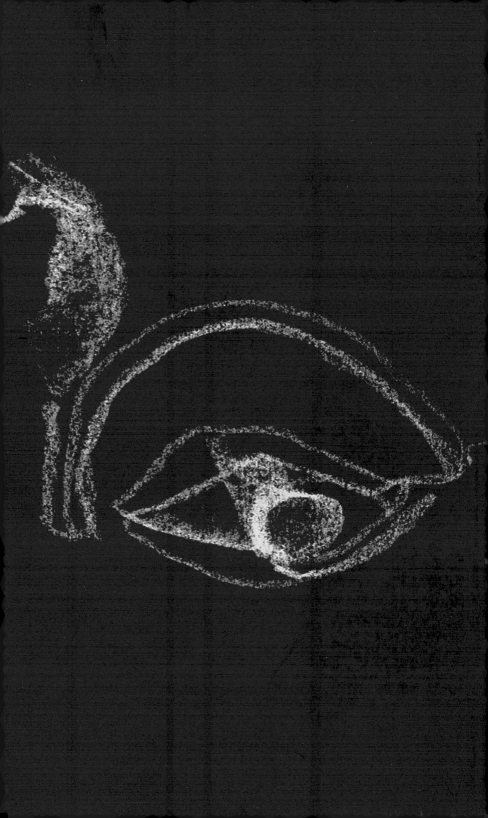